UGO FOSCOLO

———

I SEPOLCRI

Printed in Great Britain by Blackie & Son, Ltd., Glasgow

PREFACE

It was my desire to issue Foscolo's masterpiece last year on the occasion of his centenary, when the Duce of Fascismo had the happy thought to present a specially printed volume, containing a selection of the poet's verses, to "England, hospitable exile and first burying-place of the great patriot", but the heavy pressure of my teaching work rendered the task impossible.

I trust that, though the book appears late, our British friends will read with interest the poet's verses in remembrance of the veneration in which he held their country, "the noble land" that offered the poet a safe and sympathetic refuge in the days of his sorrow.

ERNESTO GRILLO.

DEPARTMENT OF ITALIAN STUDIES,
    GLASGOW UNIVERSITY,
        September, 1928.

UGO FOSCOLO

I SEPOLCRI

LIFE OF FOSCOLO

When, in 1798, Monti's opponents at Milan tried to ruin his fame and shatter his fortune, Ugo Foscolo, then a young and almost unknown poet, arose in defence of the Napoleonic singer. These two men of genius, who later became enemies through a bitter quarrel, represent brilliantly and with notable variations the uncertainties, failings and agitations of their time. Inspired by the literary and political innovations which had just been introduced into Italy, and precursors of the Romantic Revival, both of them remained indissolubly attached to the forms of classical art.

Ugo Foscolo was born in 1778 at Zante, of a Venetian father and a Greek mother. The latter, after her husband's death, settled in Venice along with her boy, who was already beginning to write verse under the influence of Alfieri, Monti, and of the Ossianic poems.

1

clergy, could suffice to quench the immortal fire that animated the Etruscans and the Latins, that fired Dante's immortal spirit amidst the sufferings of his exile, Machiavelli in the anguish of his torture, Galileo among the terrors of the Inquisition, and Tasso in his wandering life, in his persecution by the philosophers, in his long unhappy love, amidst the ingratitude of courts; unquenchable the fire not in these alone, but in countless other noble souls who suffered disaster and poverty in silence. Prostrate upon their tombs, ask the secret of their greatness and misfortune, and how their love of fatherland, of glory and of truth increased their constancy of heart, their strength of mind and the benefits they have conferred upon us."

With the abolition of this professorship Foscolo returned to Milan; but, in 1811, as there were, in the opinion of the police, unseemly allusions to Napoleon in his tragedy *Aiace*, which had been just produced at La Scala, he had to leave that city and settle in Florence. At the news of the French disasters and of the downfall of the Empire he returned to Milan, where the Austrians accorded to him a most flattering reception, and proposed that he should edit a new review, whose task would be to plead adroitly the cause of the Restoration and of the Austrian Empire. But the poet indignantly refused all their offers, and went into voluntary exile first in Switzerland and then in England.

Foscolo in London

On the 12th of September, 1816, Foscolo arrived in London. The Channel crossing was unpropitious and the unusually long sail of forty-one hours very tempestuous and dangerous. That same night another vessel foundered, and those who embarked at Calais narrowly escaped being drowned. We learn with satisfaction that, from the moment he reached England, everything was cheerful, even the pale northern sunshine; so much so that he was almost inclined to contradict those who cry out against English fogs, and to break into song with the well-known lines of his poet friend, Pindemonte:

> Non biasmi Italia più l' anglico cielo,
> Cielo che più non è gelido e scuro.

There are still extant a group of letters directed to friends and relatives which illustrate the poet's life in the British capital. " Here for the first time," he wrote to a friend, " I have perceived that I am not entirely unknown; I have been received like a man who has already enjoyed a noble and stainless reputation for a century."

The cordial and honourable welcome that Foscolo received from all those illustrious personages, who had exerted themselves to procure for him an inviolate refuge on the Thames, was such as to heal his wounds, at least for the moment. His writings were not only known but duly appreciated by people of culture,

I begin to suspect that, to escape from this grave condition, I shall have to say farewell to all literary men and noblemen, and resign myself to the bitter fate of going round to private houses teaching Italian, Latin or Greek and then of returning to my room to write for posterity; if perchance posterity will care for me. Perhaps the poverty which has terrified me has also brought me discouragement and humiliation, and I am wrong to complain that in fifty days my way of life has not been made smooth.

It is certain that in a short time I have exhausted a large part of my resources, and soon nothing will remain for me but to die, or else to become a teacher of languages. Nor should I be sorry to depart from this life, which for a long time has been so sad and painful; but what would become of my mother and of you? And how by dying a voluntary death could I compensate you and my poor mother? No help of yours could be of any avail to me; nor should I desire it. All that you, and my brother and my family could do, you have done, and far more than I should have wished. Let that suffice! Even if I allowed you to do more, it would be like drops of water on the parched ground; hence in this game that I have undertaken I must ' draw the ace or the six '."

As can be seen from this letter Foscolo's joy in the festive and unexpected welcome accorded him by the outstanding men in literature and politics was of short duration. After the legitimate satisfaction of his self-esteem, fears and uncertainties regarding the

future were not long in casting a shadow over all his hopes. The following passage from a letter to his mother is of great interest for students of Foscolo's life, and of the social and economic conditions prevailing in England at the end of the Napoleonic wars: " If I can work with profit to myself and to you, I shall stay here; if not, I shall go to Greece, where I hope I shall not lack bread; for very little will supply all my needs.

Here I have received and still receive endless welcomes, honours and flattery, but I do not foresee that they can yield me much; besides, this is a country where there are great misfortunes, and shame and despair for whomsoever requires help of others. In London, certainly, more than elsewhere, one can seize fortune by force, but whoever on the Continent thinks that here money falls like rain upon the streets is mistaken. England is full of poverty, and everything is credit and paper money, nor is a single gold sovereign seen in circulation.

You may be sure that I shall do all I can to escape from poverty and to help you. Your welfare was, and always will be, as long as I live, my first and most serious thought. Meanwhile I thank my brother and Visconti for all that they have done for me, and I would ask their pardon for all the trouble that I have given them, and for the sorrow and bitter grief that my poverty must have caused them.

My brother has little reason to counsel economy; often I have suffered and still suffer hunger. Even

when I was in more favourable circumstances I was never as rich as he thought: the nobility of my character and the dignity of my behaviour compensated for my lack of wealth; my house appears rich, and its master has the art of never seeming poor and the dignity of never wishing to seem so. But I am poor, so poor that I never go to bed at night or waken in the morning without being tortured by the painful certainty that I can do nothing for my family, nor, for the moment, can I raise a single crown to help you, poor creatures.

This state cannot last, and I repeat that very soon I shall have to decide upon a course of action. But let it not trouble you! I hope that the next letter will bring you better news of me. I wanted only to inform you of everything, so that you might not imagine that distance had changed me, or made me callous and cruel; and that my brother might know that I was forcibly compelled to impose upon him a new burden on my arrival in London. I arrived here a mere stranger, lost among the crowds, without an intimate friend, and without even a copper for a glass of water, because even water has to be dearly bought here. Farewell, my dear ones; pray God to guide and help me, above all to endure this life, that I bear so patiently for love of you—Farewell, from the bottom of my heart, farewell!"

In another letter the poet appears to be even more despondent:

" I am lonely and forsaken: at home I have no one

to help me; and it seems indeed that my mind is rusting. After a little more of this mode of life, I shall relapse into stupidity and frigid despair, because it is a necessity for me to love and be loved; and here, where I have neither friends nor relatives to bear me company, poverty forbids me to take a wife.

Alfieri writes in his Autobiography that he was never able to study except when he had near him a lover or a bosom friend—a very beautiful thing—but Alfieri never experienced the fear of having to hold out his hand to receive favours from others.''

Foscolo and Napoleon

Foscolo was fated to see Italy no more; he never again left London, where, with periods of alternating good and ill fortune, he lived by his literary labours. Towards the end of his life he retired to Turnham Green, where he died on 10th September, 1827. In 1871 his remains were brought to Florence and, with all the pomp of great national mourning, found their final resting-place in the Church of Santa Croce, beside the monuments of Machiavelli, Michael Angelo, and Galileo.

This ill-balanced, passionate character, whose weaknesses were in striking contrast with the haughtiness of his bearing and language, lacked neither courage nor nobility. His devotion to the cause of Italian liberty dominated the whole of his career; he refused to bow before the Austrian oppressors and dared

to address serious warnings to Napoleon himself.

" France," he wrote to him on one occasion, " can hope for no safety without the aid of Italy. To conquer you need the Italians and to obtain their loyal, ready help you must proclaim the independence of their fatherland. Hitherto the French have been the victors, the Italians the vanquished: the names are of no significance. But now you, O general, must adapt your politics to the times; a powerful Italian monarchy would prevent tumults in France and wars in Europe. Grant the demands for arms of the Ligurian republicans and the whole province will become a battlefield, the entire people an army.

The more sympathy you acquire in Italy, the larger will the Italian army become, for force inevitably engenders force. Then will arise the noble-minded Italians who, in former revolutions, either withdrew, or scarcely appeared, or entirely concealed themselves, scorning to submit to the tyranny of the French proconsuls and to the servile insolence of their ministers. Let these great men compose the National Italian Convention which, truly representative of a free people, will succeed in creating a constitution, which would equalize fortunes as far as possible, restore morality and convert every citizen into a soldier."

In 1803 he sent a similar appeal to the Emperor.

" To invoke you is our duty, yours is to come to our aid, not only because we share in common Latin blood, not only because the Italian revolution is your task, but so that the centuries may in silence pass over that

treaty which barters my native land, making nations suspicious and impairing the dignity of your name. Even our century could produce another Tacitus, who would commit your decision to the stern judgment of posterity."

In 1810, at the time of his quarrel with Monti, he wrote to him: " Your epitaph will sing your praises, mine will relate that, if I have many faults, my pen has ever been unsullied by lying." And, with a fine consciousness of his true worth, he wrote the following sonnet in which he paints his own portrait:

" Lined forehead, deep-set watchful eyes below
  A crop of fulvid hair; thin cheeks; a keen,
  Bold bearing; full and humorous lips, though slow
  To mirth; bowed head, broad chest, fine neck between;

  Straight limbs; in dress, taste elegant but plain;
  Steps, thoughts, acts, words, hasty to a degree;
  Prodigal, sober, honest, blunt, humane;
  Adverse to life and life adverse to me.

  Mournful most days and lone, immersed in thought,
  Incredulous in hope and fear the same;
  Love makes me cowardly, and anger brave;

  Reason with caution prompts me, but distraught
  My heart, so vile and virtuous, doth rave.
  O death, 't is thou wilt give me rest and fame."

Few predictions have been more accurately realized than this. Foscolo's writings were read with heartfelt sympathy and held in great esteem by the Italian

people on account of the depth of his sentiments and the force with which he gave vent to them. The fervid patriotism that pervades his works, and his own laborious and eventful life full of generous impulses and painful disappointments, conspired to render them very popular among the intellectual aristocracy of his age. He loved liberty and the fatherland no less than the tempestuous Alfieri, but he had not his vigorous faith in the future or his ardent enthusiasm for the great and romantic past of Italy. The poet's contempt for the present relapsed into a disconsolate pessimism embittered by the consciousness of his own worth.

Rich in vices and in virtues, as he himself said, his soul finds complete expression in his numerous letters, especially in those which show him to be less sincere than he wished to appear. Endowed with an eager mind, a passionate heart, a melancholy and impetuous disposition, Foscolo had all the gifts that make men " great and unhappy ". At the beginning of his career he finds in life no illusions, no belief either in man or in God. He finds instead the fury and the crimes of revolution; two foreign armies fiercely striving for the possession of Italy; the Italians applauding the victor, and the insolent conqueror selling the Venetian Republic like a flock of sheep.

At the age of twenty he sees the liberty of his country expire after thirteen centuries of glory; he sees her despoiled, betrayed, sold by him who proclaimed himself the liberator of the Italian peoples. This was a

great grief, the most grievous of all human woes. If the poor youth storms, curses and accuses men, who seem to him cowards, and Heaven, which seems unjust, we must not blame the sufferer, but those who are the cause of his sufferings. This sorrow embitters and tortures his youthful soul, makes him utter impetuous words, hounds him on amidst political and social events, love intrigues, sports and feats of arms. It makes him see death in everything, and desire it as repose. The only solace for this grief, the only comfort in his toilsome life, he finds in art—that plastic classical art, which was the joy of his early youth and his consolation in exile.

WORKS OF FOSCOLO

The complete series of Foscolo's works was published in Florence by Le Monnier—four volumes of *Prose Letterarie*, one of *Prose Politiche*, one volume containing *Le Ultime Lettere di Jacopo Ortis*, three volumes of Letters, two of *Saggi di Critica Storico-Letteraria*, one volume of Poems and one containing the three tragedies *Tieste*, *Aiace*, and *Ricciarda*.

An interesting volume containing a selection of Foscolo's poems was published in the autumn of last year, 1927, a copy of which was presented to the British Government by the Italian Ambassador. This special edition was issued by order of the Italian Government in Rome to commemorate the centenary of the poet's death, and the volume sent to Britain

contained a specially printed leaf bearing the following message signed by Signor Mussolini, the Italian Prime Minister: " To England, hospitable exile and first burying-place of Ugo Foscolo, the head of the Italian Government has presented this book on the centenary of the death of the Italian poet, as a mark of gratitude and as a token of the lasting spiritual fellow-feeling between the two nations."

The poet's fame now rests only on some of these literary productions. Among those worthy of note are *L' Ode a Bonaparte Liberatore*, written in 1797, in which he celebrated with great enthusiasm the triumph of democratic ideals; and the collection of Poems that he published at Pisa in 1802. This work begins with a series of admirable sonnets worthy to rank with those of Petrarch. The one entitled " A Firenze " is truly touching, and so also is that in which he painted his own portrait. Others—" A Zacinto ", " Alla Sera ", and " Alla Musa "—are full of that grace and harmony which, at the time of the Restoration, assured enduring popularity for Lamartine's *Méditations*.

Of the same period are two famous Odes, the first composed for Luigia Pallavicini on the occasion of a fall from a horse; and the other—" All' Amica Risanata "—addressed to Antonietta Fagnani convalescent after a severe illness, which reveal in all its fullness the artistic personality of the poet. In them the author appears a purely classical poet; his cult of beauty in imagery and style finds expression in a picture of restrained and firm outline, though of rather exag-

gerated perfection, whose serenity is in striking contrast with the fiery, passionate and almost romantic
temperament of the poet.

Greek mythology provides him with the elements for
his lyricism, not only in the decorative and external
part, but also in the very background and in the fiction
whereby he transforms the heroine of whom he sings
into an Olympian deity. In these light and brilliant
stanzas the transformation is effected without the least
effort; and, if some artifice is apparent, we find it in
the conception of the lyrical flights and not in their
form and technique. By birth and education Foscolo
possessed the profound intuitive intelligence of the
Greek genius; myths were for him something real and
living, and the faultless plasticity of his style is perfectly
adapted to this noble form of poetry.

Jacopo Ortis

In 1802 Foscolo issued *The Last Letters of Jacopo
Ortis*, a book which has been called a novel, but which
a recent critic styled a lyrical romance or, more simply,
a lyrical poem. Thus it seems might well be described
the substance and the form of the book. Those tortures that it makes us feel, that abrupt and jerky style,
those daring conceits and strange locutions are often
more appropriate to poetry than to prose.

Jacopo Ortis, amidst the Euganean Hills near
Padua, at the moment when Venice was handed over
to the Austrians, a prey to the discouragement that

in his ardent soul succeeds the noble illusions of patriotism, is Ugo Foscolo himself after the Treaty of Campoformio.

Under the name of Jacopo he expresses all his despair over the fate of his country and of a girl whose love might have consoled the poor exile had she not been promised to another.

His is a grief that springs from two wounds, of which the one embitters the other; and since he can hope for no consolation he ends his life by suicide. In this work there is neither dramatic action nor complicated plot; no one speaks save Jacopo alone, who describes and relates his experiences, mingling with them his sentiments, which constantly emerge as he depicts men, things and his entire self according to the state of his soul.

Ortis has been compared to Goethe's *Werther*; but these two works are as different as the two nations to which their authors belonged. *Werther* only portrays a single passion—love—and even in this the hero is not as impetuous and passionate as Ortis. The former, a man who kills himself when overcome by grief at an unrequited love, might live in any age. Ortis, on the contrary, could only have lived at that epoch when he had before him the sight of the misfortunes of his country basely betrayed at Campoformio. Werther speaks with a certain German artlessness and simplicity; Ortis finds no words adequate to express his feelings, and his language seems exaggerated to cold and indifferent men. The two books

cannot be compared, but we agree with Cesarotti that Ortis makes us forget Werther because in the *Ultime Lettere* we find more idealism and lyrical inspiration.

Foscolo's work was neither written from caprice nor to create a fine work of art, but to give vent to an unfathomable grief; it is not a romance, but a true story that bears witness to the times, and serves for moral instruction. The tone of the letters may seem to-day strange and sentimental, but the book contains many pages full of feeling and of brilliant descriptions; in it passion is strong and sincere, and the sentiments always powerfully expressed.

" Were I a painter! how ample a subject is here, for my pencil! The artist, immersed in the delightful idea of beauty, lulls to sleep or mitigates, at least, all the other passions. But even if I were a painter?—I have seen in the works of painters and poets, beautiful and sometimes unadorned nature; but nature supreme, unbounded, inimitable I have never seen painted. Homer, Dante, Shakespeare, the three masters of all those endowed with more than human genius, have taken possession of my imagination, and inflamed my heart.

I have bathed their verses with burning tears and I have adored their divine shades, as if I beheld them seated upon the lofty vaults, which overhang the universe to govern eternity. Nevertheless, the originals which I see before me, overwhelm all the powers of my soul; and I should not dare . . . I should not dare

even had Michael Angelo transfused his spirit into me, to draw even the first lines of them.

Great God! When thou beholdest a spring evening, doth thou take pleasure in thy creation? Thou hast shed upon me, for my comfort, an inexhaustible fountain of pleasure; and I have often regarded it with indifference. On the summit of the mountain gilded by the peaceful rays of the setting sun, I see myself encircled by a chain of hills, on which the harvest waves, and the vines are swayed by the breeze, sustained in rich festoons by olive and elm trees: the distant hills and the peaks of the mountains seem to grow in the distance, as if the one were laid upon the other. Beneath me, the mountain sides are split into barren cliffs; among which the evening shadows slowly rise and darken.

The bottom, obscure and horrible, appears like the mouth of a whirlpool. On the slopes towards the south, the heat of the air is mitigated by the wood, which overhangs and darkens the valley, where sheep graze in the cool shade; and she-goats, separated from the flock, climb on the rugged peaks.

The birds sing mournfully, as if they bewailed the day which is departing; young heifers low; and the wind seems to take pleasure in the whispering of the leaves. But towards the north the hills are divided, and a boundless plain is opened to the eye: the oxen, returning home, can be seen in the neighbouring fields; the weary husbandman follows them leaning on his stick; meanwhile the mothers and the wives

prepare a frugal supper for the family; the distant villas and cottages dispersed over the country can still be seen white and smoking. The shepherds milk the flock; and the old woman who sat spinning on the gate of the sheepfold leaves her work and begins to caress and stroke the bullock and the young lambs which bleat around their dams.

Meanwhile, the prospect recedes from sight; and after long successions of trees and fields, it terminates in the horizon, where the whole diminishes to the eye and blends together. The departing sun darts forth but few rays, as if those few were the last adieu which he gives to nature; the clouds become red, then fade by degrees, they pale and become grey shadows; then the plain is lost to view, shadows are diffused over the face of earth and I, as if in the midst of an ocean, see thenceforward nothing but the sky.

It was but yesterday evening that I slowly descended the hill. The world was under the guardianship of night; I heard nothing but the song of the village girl, and beheld nothing but the fires of the shepherds. All the stars twinkled, and while, one by one, I hailed the constellations, my mind acquired somewhat of a heavenly cast of thought, and my heart arose, as if it aspired to a region far more sublime than earth. I found myself on the little hill, near the church; the death-knell was tolling, and a sympathy for human nature drew my glance towards the churchyard, where beneath their grass-grown mounds the ancient fathers of the village sleep: Peace be to you, oh inanimate

relics! Matter is returned to matter: nothing diminishes, nothing increases, nothing is lost here below; all is transformed and reproduced . . . Such is the human lot! and less unhappy than others is he who does not fear it."

In *Ortis* there are also many passages in which the author challenged the most powerful leader of Europe in the zenith of his glory. The very first letter bears the date of 17th October, 1797, the day on which Napoleon signed the infamous Treaty of Campoformio. It begins with these symptomatic words: " The sacrifice of our country is completed: all is lost; and life, if indeed any be granted us, will only remain to mourn our misfortunes and our infamy." In the following letter he asks his friend: " Shall I be able to behold those who have despoiled, derided, sold us, and forbear to weep with indignation? Destroyers of the nations, they make that use of liberty which rulers made of the crusades.

Oh! if the tyrant were but one, and the vassals less stupid, my hand would suffice. What can be attempted between two powerful nations which having sworn ferocious and eternal enmity to each other, make alliance together merely to enfetter us? Where their strength is insufficient, the one deceives us with the enthusiasm for liberty; the other with the fanaticism of religion. And do we, wholly undone by our ancient servitude and our modern licentiousness, groan like vile slaves, betrayed, famished and instigated to action, neither by treachery nor by want? Alas! if it

were in my power, I would entomb my dwelling, my
dearest relatives, my friends and myself, in order
to leave absolutely nothing that would enable these
nations to boast of their powers, and of my depen-
dence."

The following passage is couched in still more violent
language:

" Let another type of Italy's lovers loudly voice their
grievance of their own accord. They complain that
they were sold and betrayed; but had they resorted
to arms, they might have been conquered, but not
betrayed; had they defended themselves and shed the
last drop of their blood, neither could the victors have
sold them, nor the vanquished dared to sell them.
And yet a great many of us suppose that money can
purchase liberty, and that foreign nations come for
love of justice to butcher each other on our fields in
order to liberate Italy! But will the French, who
have made divine liberty appear abhorrent, act like
so many Timoleons on our behalf? Not a few,
meanwhile, place their confidence in the young hero,
sprung from Italian blood and born where our sweet
idiom is spoken. For my part I shall never expect any-
thing that is noble and useful from a mind both base
and cruel. It matters not that he possesses the strength
and the roar of the lion, if his mind has the cunning of
the fox, and he is content with it, yes, a mind that is
base and cruel—nor are these epithets exaggerated.—
To what end has he refrained from selling Venice with
open and magnanimous ferocity? Selim I, who slaugh-

tered thirty thousand Circassians on the Nile, though
they had yielded to his faith, and Nadir Schah, who
in our own age massacred three hundred thousand
Indians, are more cruel, but less contemptible.

With my own eyes I saw a democratic constitution
annotated by the young hero—and sent to Venice for
acceptance—while the Treaty of Campoformio had
already been signed and ratified. Venice was bartered,
and the confidence the hero nurtured in us all has
filled Italy with banishment and exile—I do not blame
reasons of state, that sell nations like flocks of sheep:
so it has been, and so it will ever be. I weep for my
native land

That was taken from me, and still the mode offends me."

The art with which Foscolo has handled Italian
prose, in spite of some abuse of rhetoric, marks the
origin of modern prose, vigorous and vibrant with
passion. The popularity of the book was considerable;
few works, except those of Alfieri, made a more profound impression upon Italian hearts. The intense
patriotism which pervades it explains the excitement
it caused when patriotism was an offence. The mutilated copies, which escaped the censor at the beginning
of the nineteenth century, were eagerly sought after.
Young people read them; the mothers and fathers of
Italy's future warriors read them. Foscolo's life gave
increased force to his words. When all were flattering
Napoleon he had reminded the Emperor that no man
can be rightly praised till he is dead, and that his only

way of winning the praise of posterity was to establish the independence of Italy. Sooner than live under the Austrian rule he went into voluntary exile, finally taking refuge in England.

I Sepolcri

In 1807 Foscolo wrote *I Sepolcri* in most beautiful blank verse. This composition, in which the elegiac tone predominates, is neither an elegy, nor an ode, nor a poem, and, in order to give it a suitable name, the poet called it Carme. In it the sentiment of modern life and the most comprehensive patriotic emotion are fused in a form of perfect classical severity. Its chief aim is to encourage men to meditate upon the great examples whose memory is enshrined in the tombs of heroes.

> Unto what lofty deeds the spirit kindles
> Before the urns where sleep the mighty dead!
> How beautiful and holy is to the pilgrim
> The earth which guards their dust.

The poem, according to Carducci, is the only lyrical poetry Italy possesses which is Pindaric in the true sense of the word. The theme and inspiration were not new. From the history of elegiac inspiration and poetry before *I Sepolcri* in Italy, France, and especially in England through the works of Young and Gray, we learn that tombs, funereal rites, and everything pertaining to them had already formed the argument of

several prose writings, and of some poetical compositions of a learned character. It is possible that Foscolo
may have been acquainted with the works of his predecessors, but the influence of Greek poetry on his
poem appears in the Pindaric development of the
episodes, in the style which, though sometimes obscure,
is always rich in thoughts and imagery, and in his
enthusiasm for the cult of the city's gods and heroes.
Though he may have drawn upon his predecessors
Foscolo gave to his Carme an entirely original impress
by giving it a profoundly civil and patriotic conception.

The Carme was composed on the occasion of an
edict promulgated in France in 1804 and extended to
Italy in 1806, which decreed that cemeteries should be
far from the city, and that no outward sign should
differentiate the tombs of the lowly and unknown
from those of illustrious citizens. This gives to the
poet occasion for some inspired verses:

> . . . a new law removes the sepulchres
> Beyond the gaze of pity, and denies
> The dead a name. And tombless lies thy poet
> O Thalia! who, singing to thee reared
> Beneath his humble roof a laurel tree
> With long affection, garlanding thy brows.
> And thou didst brighten with thy smile the verse
> Which the Lombard Sardanapalus stung,
>
> .   .   .   .
>
> Where art thou, lonely muse? I do not feel
> The ambrosial sign of thy divinity
> Among the trees where now I sit and sigh

For my paternal home.   Here didst thou come
And smile upon him 'neath that linden tree,
That with scared leaves goes sighing to the breeze,
Because it bends not o'er the old man's urn,
To whom it once was courteous
Of calm and shadow.   Art thou wandering
Among plebeian tombs, to seek the spot
Where sleeps the sacred head of thy Parini?
No refuge to his dust the wanton city,
Patroness of effeminate singers, grants him
Within her walls—no word, no stone. . . .

Several summaries have been made of the poem.
For the convenience of the reader we reproduce below
the author's own division.

ll. 1–40. Monuments, though useless to the dead, are of
service to the living because they arouse virtuous
sentiments bequeathed by worthy men.

41–50. The wicked alone, who feel unworthy of remembrance, care not if they are forgotten.

51–90. Wrongly then does the new law banish the tombs
and all distinctions between good and evil men,
illustrious and infamous.

91–96. The funeral rites came into being along with the
social contract.

97–100. Veneration of the dead derived from the domestic
virtues.

101–104. Tombs erected to heroes through patriotism.

105–114. Superstitions and corruption from the tombs
promiscuously placed in Catholic churches.

115–136. Funeral rites of the Old Pagans and of the Modern
English.

137–150. Monuments are useless to base and corrupt nations.

151–154. The urns of heroes inspire noble deeds, and honour the cities that cherish them.

154–212. Exhortation to the Italians to reverence the tombs of their illustrious fellow-citizens in Santa Croce; their monuments will inspire them with emulation in their study and patriotism, just as the tombs of Marathon inflamed the anger of the Greeks.

212–225. The place on which the tombs of great men were erected, though now no trace of them remains, still enkindles noble hearts.

226–234. Though men of valour are persecuted while they live, and though time destroys their monuments, still the memory of their virtues and of their monuments is immortalized by writers, and lives again in the minds of those who cultivate the muses.

235–240. Witness the sepulchre of Ilus, rediscovered after many centuries by travellers whose love of letters led them to wander through the ruins of Troy.

241–257. This tomb was favoured by the gods, because it protected the body of Electra from whom descended the sons of Dardanus, the founders of Rome, and lineage of the Cæsars—masters of the world.

258–295. Episodes upon this sepulchre — Cassandra, daughter of Priam, on the tomb of the Trojan kings, predicts their immortality through the song of Homer.

While the poet in this composition deals with modern tombs he summons before our imagination the whole of Troy, the tombs of Electra, Erichthonius and Ilus, and makes us hear the lamentations of the Trojan

women and the terrible prophecies of Cassandra.
Graceful are the digressions and splendid the imagery
where, with a few masterly strokes, the artist portrays
wonderful scenes. Not without delight and admiration
do we read the eloquent allusions to Florence, with
all her glorious memories of Dante, Machiavelli and
Galileo, and proud of her temple of Santa Croce—that
true Tuscan Pantheon—where Alfieri used to muse
amidst the tombs of the illustrious dead, and thus
console himself for the cowardice of the living.

Nor are the allusions to Parini and Nelson worthy
of less praise. Fine too is the description of the won-
ders seen by those who crossed the plains of Marathon
in the silence of the night, and that of Homer groping
along towards the tombs to embrace and question them.
And how splendid is the mighty evocation of ancient
Troy, the cradle of the Trojan warriors and Roman
heroes, ending with the prophecy of Cassandra: " Troy
will perish, but Hector shall be honoured and lamented

> Wherever blood poured forth to save
> Our fatherland shall be bewailed and holy,
> As long as shines the sun on human woe."

Thus, at the moment when the poet's thoughts
seem far removed from the preoccupations of modern
life, by a natural detour he returns to the same theme.
Mythology, history, and modern ideals could not be
more intimately or more harmoniously fused. The
Carme is noteworthy for the great art by which the
poet, with a striking variety of touches, mingles the

tones of ode, canzone and hymn, of elegy and satire,
of tragedy and épopée in one sublime harmony, and
for the vast lyrical power that passes swiftly from cold
philosophical materialism to fantastic modern super-
stition, only to rise again to the serene naturalism of
the Greeks, which embraces in a rational comprehen-
sion of human history—Marathon and Santa Croce,
Aboukir and Rhætian prowess, Electra and Nelson,
Homer and Galileo.

Le Grazie

Encouraged by the success of *I Sepolcri* Foscolo
wrote several other Carmi: *L' Alceo*, *L' Oceano*, *La
Sventura*, in which he proves himself not only an
inspired poet, but also a scholar of distinction. Finally
there appeared *Le Grazie*, written amidst the fogs of
London and dedicated to Canova—a masterpiece inspired by the lovely sculptured group of the famous
Venetian artist.

Of this Carme there were at first only disconnected
and incoherent fragments. Everyone admired them
without understanding the poet's thought, until Pro-
fessor Orlandini in 1856 published the whole poem with
notes by the author himself.

To some critics *Le Grazie* seems Foscolo's most
beautiful poem—true landscape painting, sweet music,
harmonious pictorial melody—in which the poet represents the effect of the blending of physical beauty with
nobility of mind.

The Graces, participants of both heavenly and earthly glory, according to the poetical system of the author, receive from the Gods all those gifts that they are able to dispense to men. The whole mechanism of the Carme is based upon this imagery. Thus the first hymn is entitled Venus, symbolizing the beauty of the Universe; the second Vesta, image of chastity and eternal guardian of the sacred fire that inspires all gentle hearts; and the third Minerva, patron of the Arts, solace of our earthly life and teacher of mankind. In the first hymn the poet erects upon the hill of Bellosguardo, near Florence, an altar in honour of the three divinities, and invites Canova to the divine ceremony.

In the second hymn the poet transports us from ancient Greece, the first country ennobled by the Graces, to the Italy of his own day, and inaugurates a sacred festival celebrated by three Italian women, who come respectively from Milan, Bologna and Florence, and represent music, poetry and dancing. They are dear to the poet's heart, who makes them handmaids of the goddesses.

In the third hymn he sings of the ideal in art, and carries us into a delightful land, in the midst of arts so divine that ours seem hardly imitations.

Grace, the poet declares, is derived from a delicate harmony that emanates from corporal and spiritual beauty united in the highest degree of perfection within a single person. Grace ennobles and gladdens life by educating men to the divine idea of beauty,

to a delight in virtue, and to the cult of the arts, which alone can perpetuate the effects of its inspiration in the few who are thus endowed by mother nature.

PROSE WRITER AND ESSAYIST

Foscolo's merit as a prose writer lies especially in the vigour of his eloquence and in the effective expression of his critical thought. His inaugural address: " Dell' Origine e dell' Ufficio della Letteratura ", delivered at the University of Pavia in January, 1802, is noteworthy for its profound wealth of thought and solemn dignity of form. In this oration he urged his young countrymen to devote themselves to the study of letters, not from obedience to academic traditions, but for their relation to individual and national life and liberty. So great was the sensation produced by his lectures that Napoleon felt obliged to abolish all the chairs of eloquence in the Italian universities.

The polemical writings of Foscolo are subtle and full of original observations. His critical and literary prose works, the dissertation on the text of Dante and Boccaccio and that on Petrarch, published in the *Edinburgh Review*, are of considerable interest and value for the keen student of Italian literature. With Foscolo criticism took a new direction as he was one of the first to trace the origin and development of a work of art in the soul and the world of the writer, and to employ in its æsthetic appreciation the method of historical and psychological induction. The poet's ideas concerning

the nature of art are far removed both from the tra-
ditional opinion that art was the imitation and repro-
duction of the beauties of nature and from the æsthetic
materialism of the French Encyclopedists. Foscolo
moves in that sphere of idealism which art reached at the
time of the romantic revival in the nineteenth century.
The world of art for him is an entirely psychological
world, illumined by divine light and resembling a
delightful oasis in the desert of cold realism. It is the
constant aspiration after a nobler life, and through
harmony and expression exercises over the soul of
man a fascinating and tranquillizing power. The work
of art begins in the human and ends in the divine.

An entirely realistic art would no longer be art but
a feeble copy or repetition of the truth that oppresses
us; an art entirely ideal would be a phantom that our
mind could not succeed in constructing, because
memory could not supply its elements. Consequently
an artistic conception will be perfect when the real and
the ideal are so blended that one cannot tell where
the one ends and the other begins. Hence Foscolo's
admiration for Dante's finest characters, especially
Farinata, and one of the principal causes of his dis-
approval of Manzoni's tragedies, where historical and
imaginative elements are too rigidly separated.

Art is not only the idealization of reality, but also
the purification of the artist's soul. Poetry instructs
even though it does not aim at educating, because in
multiplying our sensations it multiplies our ideas.
The poet teaches in the happiest fashion by giving

the maximum wealth of ideas to the reader, and requiring the minimum exertion from him. Foscolo in addition consistently adheres to the principle that poetry is the mother of all the arts, and the mistress of the most noble artists, because it represents a mingling of music, painting, and eloquence. By analysing the other arts he concludes that poetry embodies the harmony of musical notes by means of the melody of the words, that of colour and proportion by means of images and descriptions, and the measure of verse by the harmony of forms.

Was Foscolo truly as entirely and essentially classical as we are led to believe? Were there no gaps, no weak points in his classicism? And if we asserted that, though he was not romantic, he possessed all the elements of romanticism, would our assertion be unfounded?

Speaking first of all generally, no classicist was ever wholly classical, because it is impossible for a modern man to become a thorough Latin, Greek, or pagan. The classicists were only approximately classical in varying degrees according to their greater or less measure of success in making their mode of thinking and feeling conform to the ancient mode, and their art to the ancient models. Nor was there ever a classicist, however classical, who did not accept unconsciously many moods of his time that were far from classical.

Foscolo's life and character permitted him even less than others to model himself entirely upon the ancients. He showed traces of romanticism not only

in his early years but for the whole duration of his short existence. Certain romantic tendencies more than classical were innate in him and inherent in his character, as in that of Goethe and Byron. Werther, Ortis, Harold are not only romantic personages but the first of a whole romantic family.

No young Greek or Roman would have fallen in love and killed himself like Werther and Ortis. With them Goethe and Foscolo encouraged and promoted that romantic school towards which they later changed their attitude. Goethe's novel was one of the books that kindled the imagination of Tieck. Like Werther in Germany, Ortis was in Italy one of the books most cherished by romantic youth, the one that inflicted the deepest wounds in the hearts of melancholy boys.

In both sentiment and inspiration *Le Ultime Lettere di Jacopo Ortis* is a work of romantic character. Though this epithet never actually appears in the novel, the work is full of "romantic flakes". The tone and nature of Ortis's passion, the mode of seeing and portraying life, the story of Lauretta, the idea that reason is less worthy than sentiment and inferior to it, the fusion of the author with the principal hero of the work, and not least the exaggeration of the language, that merges constantly into the lyrical and sentimental, are all purely romantic characteristics.

If here and there throughout the work we find some mythological reminiscences, if we find the names of naiads and nymphs, if Jacopo evinces enthusiasm

for Plutarch's heroes, that is not sufficient to deprive the book of its romantic character. Foscolo would certainly have been more romantic had his education not been entirely classical and if by the vicissitudes and sad experiences of his eventful life, and by the disgust at all that he saw around him, he had not been daily driven back towards antiquity. Nevertheless he remains romantic in his mode of feeling, acting, and living. His soul, capable of many contradictions, resembles a river formed by the confluence of many streams, which vary in origin, temperature and colour.

Possessed of an austere character Foscolo scorned all flattery, and never bowed before the mighty. In art he had noble thoughts and a single aim—the fatherland; he had a style all his own, which seemed at first exaggerated like his nature. His language is tinged with the colour of his times; in his later works it is purer and still more effective, because it is the incarnation of a living and vigorous thought. His genius lives and will live in his works so long as patriotism, scholarship and truly inspired poetry are held in honour.

I SEPOLCRI

I SEPOLCRI

All' ombra de' cipressi e dentro l' urne
confortate di pianto è forse il sonno
della morte men duro?   Ove piú il sole
per me alla terra non fecondi questa
5   bella d' erbe famiglia e d' animali,
e quando vaghe di lusinghe innanzi
a me non danzeran l' ore future,
né da te, dolce amico, udrò piú il verso
e la mesta armonia che lo governa,
10   né piú nel cor mi parlerà lo spirto
delle vergini Muse e dell' amore,
unico spirto a mia vita raminga,
qual fia ristoro a' dí perduti un sasso
che distingua le mie dalle infinite
15   ossa che in terra e in mar semina Morte?
Vero è ben, Pindemonte!   Anche la Speme,
ultima Dea, fugge i sepolcri; e involve
tutte cose l' obblío nella sua notte;
e una forza operosa le affatica
20   di moto in moto; e l' uomo e le sue tombe
e l' estreme sembianze e le reliquie
della terra e del ciel traveste il tempo.
Ma perché pria del tempo a sé il mortale

THE SEPULCHRES

Beneath the shade of cypresses and in tear-solaced urns will perchance the sleep of death appear less hard? When no more for me the sun shall revive this beautiful family of plants and animals, and when no 5 longer with charming flattery the coming hours shall dance before us, when from thee, sweet friend, I shall cease to hear thy mournful and melodious song, and 10 when my heart shall be for ever silent to the voice of love and of the Muses, the only comfort to my wandering life, what reward for the lost days shall then be a stone that marks my bones from those of countless crowds that death has strewn o'er land and sea? 15

Alas, Pindemonte! Even hope, our last goddess, shuns the sepulchres; in its black night oblivion enshrouds all things, and an unceasing force moves them onward through many changes, while time 20 transforms man and his tombs, our last human semblance and every trace of earth and heaven.

But why is man so prone to destroy the illusion

invidierà l' illusion che spento
25   pur lo sofferma al limitar di Dite?
    Non vive ei forse anche sotterra, quando
    gli sarà muta l' armonia del giorno,
    se può destarla con soavi cure
    nella mente de' suoi?   Celeste è questa
30   corrispondenza d' amorosi sensi,
    celeste dote è negli umani; e spesso
    per lei si vive con l' amico estinto,
    e l' estinto con noi, se pia la terra
    che lo raccolse infante e lo nutriva,
35   nel suo grembo materno ultimo asilo
    porgendo, sacre le reliquie renda
    dall' insultar de' nembi e dal profano
    piede del vulgo, e serbi un sasso il nome,
    e di fiori odorata arbore amica
40   le ceneri di molli ombre consoli.
Sol chi non lascia eredità d' affetti
    poca gioia ha dell' urna; e se pur mira
    dopo l' esequie, errar vede il suo spirto
    fra 'l compianto de' templi acherontei,
45   o ricovrarsi sotto le grandi ale
    del perdono d' Iddio; ma la sua polve
    lascia alle ortiche di deserta gleba
    ove né donna innamorata preghi,
    né passeggier solingo oda il sospiro
50   che dal tumulo a noi manda Natura.
Pur nuova legge impone oggi i sepolcri
    fuor de' guardi pietosi, e il nome a' morti
    contende.   E senza tomba giace il tuo

which, even after death, delays him upon the threshold
of the kingdom of shades?   Does he not live, even 25
there below, when the sweet harmony of day is silent
to his ears, if once more he can awaken it with tender
cares in his friend's mind?

Celestial is this loving communion with the de- 30
parted, a holy and precious gift to us. Through it we
often live with our dead friends and they with us, if
the kind earth that cradled and nourished them as 35
infants, offering them a last refuge in her maternal
bosom, preserves inviolate their relics from the raging
storms and the profane footsteps of the crowds, while
a stone keeps the remembrance of their name, and a
friendly tree consoles their ashes with the soft shadow
of its fragrant flowers.

He only who bequeaths no heritage of kind affection 40
rejoices not in his urn.   In thought he may behold his
spirit wandering on the dark shores of Acheron, or
seeking shelter beneath the mighty wings of God's 45
mercy, but his ashes he leaves to the nettles of a
deserted glebe, where no love-inspired maiden prays,
no lonely wayfarer hears the sigh that nature breathes
out from the tombs.   50

Yet to-day a new law removes the sepulchres beyond our pitiful eyes and denies the dead a name.
Without a tomb, O Thalia, lies thy poet, who, singing

sacerdote, o Talia, che a te cantando
55   nel suo povero tetto educò un lauro
con lungo amore, e t' appendea corone;
e tu gli ornavi del tuo riso i canti
che il lombardo pungean Sardanapalo,
cui solo è dolce il muggito de' buoi
60   che dagli antri abduani e dal Ticino
lo fan d' ozi beato e di vivande.
O bella Musa, ove sei tu?   Non sento
spirar l' ambrosia, indizio del tuo nume,
fra queste piante ov' io siedo e sospiro
65   il mio tetto materno.   E tu venivi
e sorridevi a lui sotto quel tiglio
ch' or con dimesse frondi va fremendo,
perché non copre, o Dea, l' urna del vecchio
cui già di calma era cortese e d' ombre.
70   Forse tu fra' plebei tumuli guardi,
vagolando, ove dorma il sacro capo
del tuo Parini?   A lui non ombre pose
tra le sue mura la città, lasciva
d' evirati cantori allettatrice,
75   non pietra, non parola; e forse l' ossa
col mozzo capo gl' insanguina il ladro
che lasciò sul patibolo i delitti.
Senti raspar fra le macerie e i bronchi
la derelitta cagna ramingando
80   su le fosse, e famelica ululando;
e uscir del teschio, ove fuggía la luna,
l' úpupa, e svolazzar su per le croci
sparse per la funerea campagna,

to thee with constant love, reared in his humble home 55
a laurel to wreathe thy brow with its branches. And
with thy smile thou didst adorn the song which stung
the Lombard Sardanapalus, whose only joy is in the
lowing of steers in the Abduan and Ticinian valleys, 60
that grace his board with feasts and luxury.

Where art thou now, O lovely Muse? I do not feel
the ambrosial symbol of thy divinity amidst these
trees where I sit longing for my maternal home. 65
Thou didst come and smile upon him beneath yon
linden tree, that with dejected leaves is mourning
because it covers not the urn of the old man, to whom
it was once courteous with peace and shade. Perhaps
thou art wandering among plebeian tombs to find 70
the spot where sleeps the sacred head of thy Parini.
No shadow, no word, no stone within her walls did
the licentious city, the lover of effeminate singers, be-
stow on him. The robber, who on the scaffold ended 75
a career of crime, may even stain the poet's bones
with the gory drops from his mutilated head.

Thou mayest hear among corruption and waste the
scratching of the wild dog that, fierce with hunger, howls 80
upon the graves; and see the hoopoe that issues from a
skull where she had fled the moonbeams, flitting away
above the crosses scattered over the funereal plain,

e l' immonda accusar col luttuoso
85 singulto i rai di che son pie le stelle
alle obbliate sepolture.   Indarno
sul tuo poeta, o Dea, preghi rugiade
dalla squallida notte.   Ah! sugli estinti
non sorge fiore ove non sia d' umane
90 lodi onorato e d' amoroso pianto.
Dal dí che nozze e tribunali ed are
dier alle umane belve esser pietose
di sé stesse e d' altrui, toglieano i vivi
all' etere maligno ed alle fere
95 i miserandi avanzi che Natura
con veci eterne a sensi altri destina.
Testimonianza a' fasti eran le tombe,
ed are a' figli; e uscían quindi i responsi
de' domestici Lari, e fu temuto
100 su la polve degli avi il giuramento:
religïon che con diversi riti
le virtú patrie e la pietà congiunta
tradussero per lungo ordine d' anni.
Non sempre i sassi sepolcrali a' templi
105 fean pavimento; né agl' incensi avvolto
de' cadaveri il lezzo i supplicanti
contaminò; né le città fur meste
d' effigïati scheletri: le madri
balzan ne' sonni esterrefatte, e tendono
110 nude le braccia su l' amato capo
del lor caro lattante, onde nol desti
il gemer lungo di persona morta
chiedente la venal prece agli eredi

and upbraiding with her mournful cry the rays that
the merciful stars cast on the long-forgotten tombs. 85
In vain, O Goddess, thou prayest the cheerless nights
to shed their dew upon thy poet. Alas, over the dead
there grows no flower that is not honoured by warm
love and human tears.   90

From the day when marriage, tribunals and temples
caused the human brutes to be merciful to themselves
and to others, the living protected from injury of the
air and from wild beasts the miserable remains which 95
nature with its eternal changes to other purposes
destines.

Tombs were then monuments to the people's heroism
and altars for their children; thence came the answers
of the household gods, and oaths taken on the fore-
fathers' ashes were deemed sacred; this was a religion, 100
which with different rites through a long course of
years, preserved unstained both civil virtues and love
for their parents.

Not always did sepulchral stones pave our temples, 105
nor did the foul smell of corpses, mingled with the
fuming incense, poison the worshippers, nor were our
cities saddened by effigies of ghastly skeletons. Behold mothers terrified by dreadful dreams stretch
forth their naked arms upon the head of their dear 110
infants, lest they may be awakened by the deep moan
of the restless dead seeking a mercenary prayer from
the ministers of the sanctuary. But cypresses and

nelle adulate reggie ha sepoltura
145   già vivo, e i stemmi unica laude. A noi
morte apparecchi riposato albergo,
ove una volta la fortuna cessi
dalle vendette, e l' amistà raccolga
non di tesori eredità, ma caldi
150   sensi e di liberal carme l' esempio.
    A egregie cose il forte animo accendono
l' urne de' forti, o Pindemonte; e bella
e santa fanno al peregrin la terra
che le ricetta.   Io quando il monumento
155   vidi ove posa il corpo di quel grande,
che, temprando lo scettro a' regnatori,
gli allòr ne sfronda, ed alle genti svela
di che lagrime grondi e di che sangue;
e l' arca di colui che nuovo Olimpo
160   alzò in Roma a' celesti; e di chi vide
sotto l' etereo padiglion rotarsi
piú mondi e il sole irradïarli immoto,
onde all' anglo, che tanta ala vi stese,
sgombrò primo le vie del firmamento;
165   Te beata, gridai, per le felici
aure pregne di vita e pe' lavacri
che da' suoi gioghi a te versa Apennino!
Lieta dell' aer tuo veste la luna
di luce limpidissima i tuoi colli
170   per vendemmia festanti, e le convalli
popolate di case e d' oliveti
mille di fiori al ciel mandano incensi:
e tu prima, Firenze, udivi il carme

in their famed palaces, and their emblems are their 145
only praise. For us death may provide a place of rest
where once for ever fortune ceases to be vindictive
and friendship enjoys not an inheritance of treasures,
but warm feelings of love and the example of an inspired song. 150

The urns of heroes, O Pindemonte, with mighty
deeds inspire the noble souls, and holy and beautiful
for the pilgrim is the earth that holds them. When I
beheld the monument of that immortal, who tempering 155
the rulers' sceptres tore off their laurel and to the
world revealed the tears and the blood which stains
them; and the arch of the genius who reared in Rome
to the celestials a new Olympus, and that of him who 160
saw new worlds revolve beneath the ethereal vault,
and the sun motionless flooding them with light,
whereby he first cleared the paths of heaven for the
daring Briton who flew so high, how happy art thou,
O Tuscany, I exclaimed, with thy breezes full of life 165
and with the streams which from their rugged peaks
the Apennines pour down upon thee! Rejoicing in
thy air the moon invests with its silvery light thy hills
smiling with vine trees, while thy happy valleys dotted 170
with villas and olive groves send forth to heaven the
fragrance of a thousand flowers.

And first, O Florence, didst thou hear the song that

che allegrò l' ira al ghibellin fuggiasco;
175   e tu i cari parenti e l' idïoma
desti a quel dolce di Calliope labbro
che Amore, in Grecia nudo e nudo in Roma,
d' un velo candidissimo adornando,
rendea nel grembo a Venere celeste.
180   Ma piú beata, ché in un tempio accolte
serbi l' itale glorie, uniche forse,
da che le mal vietate Alpi e l' alterna
onnipotenza delle umane sorti
armi e sostanze t' invadeano ed´are
185   e patria e, tranne la memoria, tutto.
Che ove speme di gloria agli animosi
intelletti rifulga ed all' Italia,
quindi trarrem gli auspicî.   E a questi **marmi**
venne spesso Vittorio ad ispirarsi.
190   Irato a' patrii numi, errava muto
ove Arno è piú deserto, i campi e il cielo
desïoso mirando; e poi che nullo
vivente aspetto gli molcea la cura,
qui posava l' austero, e avea sul volto
195   il pallor della morte e la speranza.
Con questi grandi abita eterno, e l' ossa
fremono amor di patria.   Ah sí! da **quella**
religïosa pace un nume parla;
e nutría contro a' Persi in Maratona,
200   ove Atene sacrò tombe a' suoi prodi,
la virtú greca e l' ira.   Il navigante,
che veleggiò quel mar sotto l' Eubea,
vedea per l' ampia oscurità scintille

softened the anger of the exiled Ghibelline, and
parents and speech didst thou grant to that sweet lip 175
of Calliope, who adorning with a pure white veil Love
that had appeared naked in Greece and Rome, restored
him to the bosom of celestial Venus.

But even more blessed art thou because in a temple 180
thou guardest the Italian glories, the only glories since
the unprotected Alps and the all-powerful vicissitudes
of human events deprived thee of arms, treasures,
altars, fatherland—of all except memory.   185

But wherever hope of redemption fills the heart of
Italy and of her valiant souls thence shall we draw our
omens. To these monuments often did Alfieri come
in quest of inspiration; wroth with his country's gods 190
he wandered silent over Arno's most deserted banks,
anxiously gazing on the fields and sky; and when
no living object softened his cares, here the austere
man rested, showing on his countenance the pallor of
death and a flickering of hope.   195

With these great spirits he now abides eternally and
his bones quiver with the love of Italy.

Ah yes, from that divine peace a God is speaking;
the same who nourished the flame of Grecian valour
and anger against the Persians at Marathon, where
grateful Athens reared tombs to her heroes. The 200
traveller who sailed on the Eubæan sea through the
vast darkness descried the flashing of helmets and

balenar d' elmi e di cozzanti brandi,
205   fumar le pire igneo vapor, corrusche
d' armi ferree vedea larve guerriere
cercar la pugna e all' orror de' notturni
silenzi si spandea lungo ne' campi
di falangi un tumulto, e un suon di tube,
210   e un incalzar di cavalli accorrenti
scalpitanti su gli elmi a' moribondi,
e pianto, ed inni, e delle Parche il canto.
Felice te che il regno ampio de' venti,
Ippolito, a' tuoi verdi anni correvi!
215   E se il pilota ti drizzò l' antenna
oltre l' isole egèe, d' antichi fatti
certo udisti suonar dell' Ellesponto
i liti, e la marea mugghiar portando
alle prode retèe l' armi d' Achille
220   sovra l' ossa d' Aiace: a' generosi
giusta di glorie dispensiera è morte;
né senno astuto, né favor di regi
all' Itaco le spoglie ardue serbava,
ché alla poppa raminga le ritolse
225   l' onda incitata dagl' inferni Dei.
E me che i tempi ed il desío d' onore
fan per diversa gente ir fuggitivo,
me ad evocar gli eroi chiamin le Muse
del mortal pensiero animatrici.
230   Siedon custodi de' sepolcri; e quando
il tempo con sue fredde ale vi spazza
fin le rovine, le Pimplèe fan lieti
di lor canto i deserti, e l' armonia

the clashing of swords, he saw the dense smoke of
funereal pyres, the glittering of warrior ghosts in steel 205
armour seeking the fray, while along the battlefield
through the horror of the nocturnal silence, was heard
the tumult of legions, the blast of trumpets, the charge
of rushing steeds trampling upon the helmets of the 210
dying warriors, and wailings, hymns, and the song of
the three fates.

Happy art thou, O Pindemonte, that in thy green
years hast travelled through the boundless kingdom
of the winds, and if thy pilot sailed beyond the 215
Ægean Islands, thou certainly didst hear the shores of
Hellespont resound with ancient deeds, and how the
roaring waves brought to the Rhætian land Achilles' 220
arms upon the bones of Ajax: to the generous death
is a just arbiter of glory; neither cunning art, nor
royal act of grace preserved for Ulysses the hard-won
spoils, for the roaring sea moved by infernal gods
stole them away from the wandering bark.   225

And me, whom perverse times and thirst for glory
caused to be a fugitive through many foreign lands,
may the Muses, inspirers of every human thought,
call to evoke the fame of every mighty hero.

They are enthroned as guardians of the sepulchres; 230
and when time with its cold wings sweeps away even
the ruins, the Pimplean singers will gladden the desert

vince di mille secoli il silenzio.

235 Ed oggi nella Troade inseminata
eterno splende a' peregrini un loco;
eterno per la ninfa a cui fu sposo
Giove, ed a Giove diè Dàrdano figlio,
onde fur Troia e Assàraco e i cinquanta
240 talami e il regno della Giulia gente.
Però che quando Elettra udí la Parca
che lei dalle vitali aure del giorno
chiamava a' cori dell' Eliso, a Giove
mandò il voto supremo, e: Se, diceva,
245 a te fur care le mie chiome e il viso
e le dolci vigilie, e non mi assente
premio miglior la volontà de' fati,
la morta amica almen guarda dal cielo,
onde d' Elettra tua resti la fama.
250 Cosí orando moriva. E ne gemea
l' Olimpio; e l' immortal capo accennando
piovea dai crini ambrosia su la ninfa,
e fe' sacro quel corpo e la sua tomba.
Ivi posò Erittonio, e dorme il giusto
255 cenere d' Ilo; ivi l' iliache donne
sciogliean le chiome, indarno ahi! deprecando
da' lor mariti l' imminente fato;
ivi Cassandra, allor che il nume in petto
le fea parlar di Troia il dí mortale,
260 venne; e all' ombre cantò carme amoroso,
e guidava i nepoti, e l' amoroso
apprendeva lamento a' giovinetti.

.with their songs and their harmony will overcome the
silence of a thousand centuries.

To-day in Troy's untilled soil before the pilgrim's 235
eyes shines for ever a place immortalized by the
nymph, who was Love's bride, Dardanus' mother,
whence descended Troy and Assaracus, the fifty
nuptials of Priam's sons and the great kingdom of 240
the Julian race.

But when Electra heard the decree of death, which
from the vital light of day called her to the Elysian
chorus, to Jupiter she sent her last request: " And
if," she said, " my face and hair, and our sweet vigils
were ever dear to thee, since fate does not grant me 245
a better lot, at least from heaven protect thy departed
friend, so that thy Electra's fame may live."

Thus praying she died. The Olympian deity sighed 250
and assenting with immortal head poured from his hair
ambrosia upon the nymph and consecrated both her
body and her tomb. Here were buried Erichthonius and
the ashes of just Ilus; here Troy's daughters unbound 255
their locks vainly deprecating their husband's impend-
ing doom.

Here came Cassandra when the god that agitated
her heart made her foretell Troy's fatal day; unto 260
these spirits she chanted a loving song; here she led
her young descendants and taught them her mournful

E dicea sospirando: Oh se mai d' Argo,
ove al Tidide e di Laerte al figlio
265 pascerete i cavalli, a voi permetta
ritorno il cielo, invan la patria vostra
cercherete!   Le mura, opra di Febo,
sotto le lor reliquie fumeranno.
Ma i Penati di Troia avranno stanza
270 in queste tombe; ché de' numi è dono
servar nelle miserie altero nome.
E voi, palme e cipressi, che le nuore
piantan di Priamo, e crescerete, ahi presto
di vedovili lagrime innaffiati,
275 proteggete i miei padri: e chi la scure
asterrà pio dalle devote frondi,
men si dorrà di consanguinei lutti,
e santamente toccherà l' altare.
Proteggete i miei padri.   Un dí vedrete
280 mendico un cieco errar sotto le vostre
antichissime ombre, e brancolando
penetrar negli avelli, e abbracciar l' urne,
e interrogarle.   Gemeranno gli antri
secreti, e tutta narrerà la tomba
285 Ilio raso due volte e due risorto
splendidamente su le mute vie
per far piú bello l' ultimo trofeo
ai fatati Pelidi.   Il sacro vate,
placando quelle afflitte alme col canto,
290 i prenci argivi eternerà per quante
abbraccia terre il gran padre Oceàno.

melody.   And sighing she said: "Oh if from the
Grecian shores, where you shall feed Achilles' and
Ulysses' chargers, heaven will ever grant you to return, 265
vainly you will seek your fatherland; the walls which
Phœbus built will fume beneath their ruins.   But
Troy's gods shall abide within these tombs; for it is a 270
gift of heaven to preserve an honoured name in the
midst of miseries. And ye palms and cypresses, which
Priam's daughters have planted soon to grow watered
by the widow's tears, protect my fathers. And he who 275
with reverence will restrain his axe from the sacred
branches shall feel less the grief of his kinsman's
mourning, and holy shall he come unto this altar.
Protect my fathers.

One day ye shall see an old blind beggar wander- 280
ing beneath your ancient shadows, groping there to
penetrate within the sepulchres and kiss the urns and
question them. The hidden caves shall groan and the
tombs shall relate the tale of Ilium twice laid waste and 285
twice rebuilt with new splendour on the silent plain
to adorn the last trophy of Peleus' sons. The sacred
poet, consoling with his song those afflicted spirits,
shall render immortal the Argivian princes through 290
all the lands encircled by great Father Ocean. And

E tu onore di pianti, Ettore, avrai
ove fia santo e lagrimato il sangue
per la patria versato, e finché il sole
295   risplenderà su le sciagure umane.

thou, Hector, shalt have the honour of tears wherever blood shed for the redemption of our fatherland shall be bewailed and holy, as long as the sun shines on human woes. 295